NEVADA MOMENTS: WHISPERS IN THE WIND

This is a record of moments in light and moments in life, not a chronicle
of tourist attractions and celebrities.

Nevada quotations are from Mark Twain's "Roughing It" and his letter
to the California Pioneers. They are matched to photos to underscore
a common thread, not for geographic accuracy.

Nevada's topography and climate are punctuated by extremes. Its people
are strong and self-effacing individuals inspired by place and possibilities.

To all who contributed their character and ideas to this book, thank you.

NEVADA MOMENTS
Whispers in the Wind

PHOTOGRAPHS BY DANIEL WIENER

WIT AND WISDOM BY MARK TWAIN

"At rare intervals - but very rare - there were clouds in our skies,

and then the setting sun would gild and flush and glorify this

mighty expanse of scenery with a bewildering pomp of color

that held the eye like a spell and moved the spirit like music."

Near Copper Canyon

"... it was not very long before night came - and not with a lingering

twilight, but with a sudden shutting down like a cellar door, as is

its habit in that country."

Shoshone Range and the Reese River Valley

Reese River Valley and Shoshone Range

Old snag, Mount Charleston

Terri Zelenak, teacher, John C. Fremont Middle School, Las Vegas

St. Mary's in the Mountains, Virginia City

"It flicked like a candle-flame, and looked no larger;

but with such a background, it was wonderfully bright,

small as it was. It was the flag."

Renada Neroes, Las Vegas

"Visibly our new home was a desert, walled in by barren, snow-clad mountains. There was not a tree in sight. There was no vegetation but the endless sage-brush and greasewood."

Near Rachel

"The eye was never tired of gazing, night or day, in calm or storm;

it suffered but one grief, and that was that it could not look

always, but must close sometimes in sleep."

Emma Workman, Ely

". . .we watched the sentinel peaks put on the glory of the sun, and

followed the conquering light as it swept down among the shadows,

and set the captive crags and forests free."

North Peak near Valmy

"I had grown well accustomed to wearing a damaged slouch hat,

blue woolen shirt, and pants crammed into boot-tops,

and gloried in the absence of coat, vest and braces."

Rancher Jim Berg, Carver's

Marvel Ranch, Paradise Valley

East of Winnemucca

"On the seventeenth day, we passed the highest mountain peaks

we had yet seen, and although the day was very warm the night

that followed upon its heels was wintry cold

and blankets were next to useless."

North of Golconda

Anna Nunez, Las Vegas

Valley of Fire State Park

"He was one of the best and kindest hearted men

that ever graced a humble sphere of life. He was gentleness

and simplicity itself - and unselfishness, too."

Joe Leonard, Battle Mountain

Justin Johnston, Cherry Pizzarelle, Hadley

George Maxwell, Pete Coscarart make chorizo sausage, Lemaire's General Store, Battle Mountain

"We were stark mad with excitement - drunk with happiness -

smothered under mountains of prospective wealth - arrogantly

compassionate toward the plodding millions who knew not our

marvellous canyon - but our credit was not good at the grocer's."

The Manhattan Bar

". . . one could look over a vast, far-reaching panorama of mountain ranges

and deserts; and whether the day was bright or overcast, whether the sun was

rising or setting, or flaming in the zenith, or whether night when the moon

held sway, the spectacle was always impressive and beautiful."

Toiyabe Range and Smoky Valley

"It nestled in the edge of a great plain and was a sufficient number of miles

away to look like an assemblage of mere white spots in the shadow of a grim

range of mountain overlooking it, whose summits seemed lifted clear out

of companionship and consciousness of earthly things."

Las Vegas at dusk

Leon Shelton, sauce cook, Sahara Hotel, Las Vegas

Alta Wilson dismantles 105 mm projectiles, Hawthorne

Old truck, Minden

Cattle grazing before approaching storm, Dunphy

"The Washoe Zephyr (Washoe is a pet nickname for Nevada)

is a peculiarly Scriptural wind, in that no man knoweth 'whence it cometh.'

It comes right over the mountains from the West, but when one crosses the ridge

he does not find any of it on the other side! It probably is manufactured

on the mountaintop for the occasion, and starts from there."

Storm over the Toiyabe Range, Hadley

"Of all the experiences of my life, this secret search among the hidden

treasures of silver-land was the nearest to unmarred ecstasy.

It was a delirious revel. By and by, in the bed of a shallow rivulet, I found

a deposit of shining yellow scales, and my breath almost forsook me!

A gold mine, and in my simplicity I had been content with vulgar silver!"

Round Mountain Gold Mine

"Presently I found a bright fragment and my heart bounded!

I hid behind a boulder and polished it and scrutinized

it with a nervous eagerness and a delight that was more pronounced

than absolute certainty itself could have afforded.

The more I examined the fragment the more I was convinced

that I had found the door to fortune."

Refiner Kiko Herrera and gold bars, Round Mountain Gold Mine

Israel Fimbres, Battle Mountain

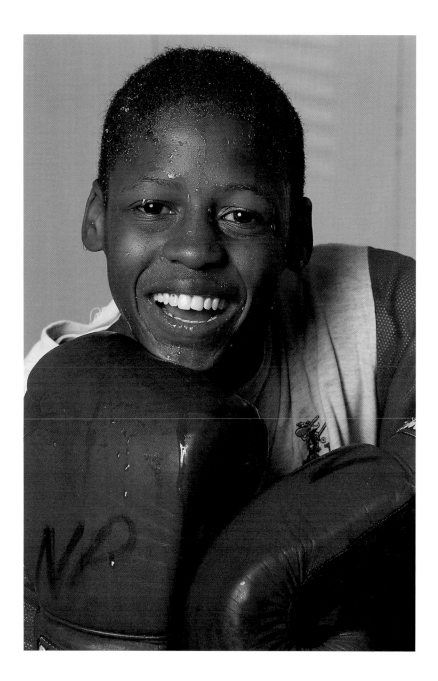

Clint Harvey at Nevada Partners Gym, North Las Vegas

Loader working at heap leach pad, Round Mountain Gold Mine

Airport, Battle Mountain

"There are several rivers in Nevada, and they all have this mysterious fate. They end in various lakes or 'sinks,' and that is the last of them. Carson Lake, Humboldt Lake, Walker Lake, Mono Lake, are all great sheets of water without any visible outlet. Water is always flowing into them; none is ever seen to flow out of them, and yet they remain always level full, neither receding nor overflowing. What they do with their surplus is only known to the Creator."

Walker Lake

"We shivered in the lee of a boulder all the rest the of day, and froze all the night through."

Pogonip-covered sage along the Humboldt River, Carlin

Cemetery, Belmont

Telegraph pole along the Union Pacific, east of Gerlach

"Finally I walked home - 200 miles - partly for exercise, and

partly because stage fare was expensive."

Highway 50 at Major's Place

" . . . all about us the white glare of the snow-bed enabled us to

discern the smooth sugar-loaf mounds made by

the covered sage bushes, and just in front of us the two faint

grooves which we knew were the steadily filling

and slowly disappearing wheel-tracks."

"Gentlemen, I have planned a lucrative and useful

service for you - a service which will provide you with recreation

amid noble landscapes and afford you never ceasing opportunities

for enriching your minds by observation and study."

Jerry Pierce and Estaban Salazar, Hadley

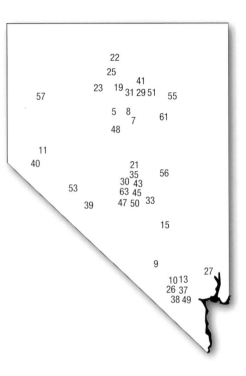

Credits

Design
Ronan Kearney
Signa Design Communications Inc.
Montreal, QC

Scanning
Imagetech, Montreal, QC

Film & Imposition
Tri-Graphiques, Montreal, QC

Printing
Friesens, Altona, MB

Distribution
Priorities
832 Gold Court
Battle Mountain, NV 89820

ISBN Number 1-55056-518-4

Printed in Canada